B.R.3/2

BRITISH TRANSPORT COMMISSION
BRITISH RAILWAYS
.... L.M. .... REGION

FROM District Motive Power Supt.,
Kentish Town.

| OUR REF. | K.31/3 |
| DATE | 21.6.60 |

(Centre No. 100)

| YOUR REF. | |
| DATED | |

(Centre No.)   Extn.

TO Driver A. Chambers,
Kentish Town.

FOOTPLATE PERMITS.

Please note that permission has been g...
C.P. Walker to travel on the footplate of the loc...
the 2/25 from Manchester to St.Pancras on 24th Ju...
Leicester and St.Pancras.

85, Steetley Lane,
Tottenham, N.15.
12th July 1960.

Dear Mr. Walker,

Thank you very much for your letter & photographs. The photos are quite good, really, considering the weather. I am glad you enjoyed the trip. I hope to have the pleasure of your company again on some future occasion.

You will find enclosed the Memo that was given to me with reference to your trip. I shall be pleased to you will accept it as a small "memento".

Regarding my own particular link: at the moment my own particular link is at the "Sixes & Sevens" due to the introduction of the Midland Pullman, which makes it impossible for me to be settled for some little while yet.

However, if there is anything I can do to help from this end perhaps you will let me know and I shall be only too pleased to try.

Many thanks, once again, for your letter and photographs.

Yours sincerely
J.A. Chambers.

LONDON MIDLAND STEAM TWILIGHT
Part One

Frontispiece. *On Sunday, July 31st 1960 a 'Britannia' Pacific No 70033 'Charles Dickens' from Trafford Park depot in Manchester is 'borrowed' by Nottingham shed to work the 7.40 am Sunday train to London. After arriving at St. Pancras it waits at the buffer stops in Platform 7 while the empty stock is removed by a 2-6-4 tank.*

LONDON MIDLAND STEAM TWILIGHT

Midland lines and the
Somerset and Dorset
Part One

Colin Walker

PENDYKE PUBLICATIONS

INTRODUCTION

This book is the first of two albums from the author's personal collection of photographs recalling steam working over the Midland lines of the former London Midland Region of British Railways. Also included are linked routes that were 'lost' to other Regions after nationalisation like those into Sheffield and the Bristol main line south of Birmingham together with the Somerset & Dorset out of Bath which were all lines where London Midland engines continued to operate.

This, and Book Two will cover the same areas and often the same locations but each will contain a different selection of photographs. If there is something of an emphasis on photographs taken in and around Leicestershire then this arises naturally from the author's lengthy residence in that part of the world.

When so much of the nation's heavy industry has now been 'shed' to other, cheaper parts of the world and the fuels we use for most of our heating and manufacture are met from our resources of oil, natural gas and generated electricity we should not forget that in the days of our industrial prowess and prosperity it was metals like iron and steel and fuels like coal and coke that underpinned a large portion of the national economy. Central to this success and prosperity were the railways and the coal, ore and steel trains that still continued to ply the tracks in the late 1950s and early 60s were the last representatives of a long and impressive tradition. In this the Midland lines made a massive contribution. Now, except for coal to power stations and concentration depots and coils of sheet steel for special treatments like tube-making, the numerous train loads of coal, steel and indigenous iron-ore as featured in this book are, like the steam locomotives that hauled them all things of the past. So too are many of the lines they travelled.

The author wishes to acknowledge the former London Midland Region of British Railways for their generous photographing facilities. Remembered too are the numerous signalmen, station, yard and permanent way staff who co-operated and connived in his pursuit of interesting photography. Also warmly remembered are the many, many enginemen who officially and unofficially found room for him and all his 'gear' on their footplates. They were all a pleasure to know.

Finally, he also wishes to thank Tom Pepper, Administration Manager of 'City Bus' (formerly Leicester City Transport) for unearthing details of the bus that toppled over in 1946. He can now retire in peace.

ISBN 0904318 16 8

© Colin Walker 1995

Published by:
Pendyke Publications,
Methodist Hill,
Froncysyllte,
Llangollen,
Clwyd.
LL20 7SN.

Tel/Fax 01691 778180

Photoset in North Wales by Derek Doyle & Associates, Mold, Clwyd.
Printed by The Amadeus Press Ltd, Huddersfield, W Yorkshire.

2. *A month earlier on the 24th June 1960 a 'Royal Scot' No 46133 'The Green Howards' stands in platform 4 at St. Pancras having arrived with the up 'Palatine' from Manchester Central.*

3. *Kentish Town top link driver Jim Chambers and his willing fireman Tony Goodwin who brought No 46133 into St. Pancras right time in spite of a string of permanent way slowings near Wilshampstead. 24.6.60.*

4. *'Royal Scot' No 46133 'The Green Howards' heading the up 'Palatine' from Manchester gathers speed again after slowing for bridge renewal works near Wilshampstead. 24.6.60.*

Previous Page

5. Two Jubilees' Nos 45667 'Jellicoe' and 45712 'Victory' back down to St. Pancras station from Kentish Town shed and hook on to the 2.25pm express to Manchester Central in Platform 7. No 45667 will not be assisting 'Victory' however, but instead after detaching, will move over to Platform 4 where she will couple up to the 3.10pm express to Bradford Forster Square via Melton Mowbray and Nottingham.

6. Kettering. The spire of Kettering's parish church of Saints Peter & Paul dominates the skyline as a Stanier 'Black 5' 4-6-0 No 44811 hurries away from the town with the 1.45pm local to Leicester London Rd. via Oakham and Melton Mowbray.

7. An 8F No 48356 running tender first takes a train of iron ore for Corby steel works along the down Nottingham line north of Kettering.

8. 'Britannia' Pacific No 70033 'Charles Dickens' sets out from Desborough and Rothwell after calling with the Sunday 7.40 am from Nottingham to St. Pancras. 31.7.60.

9. No 70033's driver Joe Simpson from Nottingham awaits the guard's 'right away' from Kettering. 31.7.60.

10. *'Jubilee' No 45590 'Travancore' pulls away from Market Harborough and begins the 4½ mile climb of Desborough bank with the 7.40am express from Sheffield to St. Pancras. 1.8.59.*

11. *'Travancore's crew, Driver Frank Elliott and his fireman Dennis Polkey from Sheffield's Millhouses depot. Notice the advice on the cab roof about the detection of an overheating middle big end which set off a warning odour similar to garlic. Driver Elliott's father, Jack, was also a driver at Sheffield Millhouses. 1.8.59.*

12. *Market Harborough was an interesting cross roads where the former L.N.W. lines from Northampton and Rugby to Peterborough and Melton Mowbray crossed the Midland main line from St. Pancras to Leicester and the north. Here a Northampton 8F No 48440 pauses to take water before continuing its journey over the G.N/L.N.W. Joint line with the 12.45pm Blisworth-Frodingham iron ore train. 5.9.61.*

13. *Under way. 8F No 48440 heads down the gradient from Market Harborough with the heavily loaded 12.45pm iron ore train from Blisworth to Frodingham. It is about to pass beneath the Midland main line after which it will take the G.N./L.N.W. Joint line eastwards into High Leicestershire. 5.9.61.*

14. *A Colwick 'Austerity' 2-8-0 No 90492 arrives in Welham sidings near Market Harborough on the G.N./L.N.W. Joint line with a train load of coal from the Nottinghamshire pits bound for Sudbury Junction in London. It will briefly 'associate' with the Midland main line at Market Harborough before taking the route across to Northampton. 5.9.61.*

15. *After being slowed by a 'distant on' approaching Market Harborough 'Royal Scot' No 46133 'The Green Howards' opens up again with the up 'Palatine'. 24.6.60.*

16. *A photograph taken on May 2nd 1959 finds a Burton on Trent 'Crab' 2-6-0 No 42855 cheerfully clanking down the gradient from Kibworth with the returning beer empties from London.*

17. *Over a year later on 27th July 1960 a Wellingborough 9F revels in some high spirits and speed as she storms down the grade between Wistow and Great Glen with the 10.53 am Saturday holiday train from Hastings to Leicester London Road. The train is composed of Southern Region stock.*

18. *Judging from its 'kempt' appearance Toton 8F No 48271 has recently returned from a 'shopping'. It is seen with an up coal train heading*

19. In the other direction a 'Jubilee' No 45614 'Leeward Islands' hurries north over the 'hump' near Great Glen with the 12.15pm from St. Pancras to Bradford Forster Square.

Following Page. 20. This photograph appeared in a previous book of mine but is a particular favourite and well worthy of some double page treatment not least because of the images and sounds it arouses in the memory. Stanier 'Jubilee' No 45675 'Hardy' is seen storming the rise near Wistow with the up 'Thames Clyde Express' on 2nd May 1959. Like the 'Waverley' express from Edinburgh, the 'Thames-Clyde' running between Glasgow St. Enoch and St. Pancras involved a long and arduous run despite breaks for an engine change at both Carlisle and Leeds. If time was lost, (and it often was), it was not easy to recover. On the day this photograph was taken the express was 10 minutes down at Leicester and 'Hardy's' crew were captured throwing everything the engine had got into a massive effort to recover the arrears. The sight and sound of a finely styled steam locomotive being so thoroughly extended was quite invigorating and how vividly one remembers the way the lungs filled up with that deep intake of appreciation after the train had passed. This was steam triumphant.

21. On a bright Autumn afternoon a Standard Class 2 Mogul No 78020 makes heavy weather of the 1 in

22. A 'Britannia' No 70014 'Iron Duke' from Trafford Park depot in Manchester passes Kilby Bridge on a

deconstruction of its Dome arch.) some Western Division trains from Manchester London Road were diverted into St. Pancras. Here a 'Jubilee' from Manchester's Longsight depot, No 45638 'Zanzibar' approaches Kilby Bridge with the 12 noon express from Manchester London Road. 28.12.59.

24. *Double heading to keep time. A Stanier Class 5 4-6-0 No 45101 from Newton Heath depot in Manchester provides assistance for a 'Jubilee' as they hurry down the grade towards Wigston with the 1.55pm from St. Pancras to Manchester London Road.*

Jubilee No 45650 'Blake' gathers speed round the curve between Wigston and Kilby bridge with a Christmas extra for St. Pancras.

December 1958

through Wigston Magna station with the the up 'Palatine' on Easter Monday 1960.

Regiment' in fine condition drifts past the signal box at Wigston South Junction with the 10.35am from St. Pancras to Manchester Central.

28. *A precarious shot from the top of the water tower at Wigston Junction catches two 'Black 5's' Nos 44985 and 44842 double heading a late running 'Thames*

29. *The driver of Stanier 8F 2-8-0 No 48306 which is waiting for the road with an up coal train at Wigston South Junction stands to watch 'Black 5' 4-6-0 No*

30. Stanier Class 5 No 44717 puts a smoke screen over Wigston South Junction box as it hurries south with the 9.40 am Sunday train from Manchester Central to

31. A northbound ironstone train passes Wigston South Junction on the down

32. On a hot afternoon in July 1960 another 'Black 5' No 44985 runs cautiously past Wigston North Junction with the up 'Thames-Clyde Express'

33. The Leicester-Rugby branch. This was the original Midland Counties route to London Euston and was built in 1840 well before the other routes appeared hence its almost straight course compared with the later lines. Here, a Rugby Fairburn 2-6-4 tank No 42061 parts company with the Nuneaton and Birmingham line and approaches South Wigston station with the 5.45 pm from

34. *Leicester Midland Driver Ralph Leedham and his fireman Maurice Wood on Fowler 4P 2-6-4 tank No 42352 working the 4.20 pm local from Leicester to Rugby . A short time after this photograph was taken Ralph Leedham was tragically killed on the Burton branch while shovelling coal forward in his engine's tender during which operation his head hit an overbridge. This was most probably the last photograph ever taken of him.*

35. *It was an operating custom at Leicester Midland to work its tank engines to Rugby bunker first and back engine first. Here Fowler 4P tank No 42352 sets off from Broughton Astley with the 4.20 pm local train from Leicester London Road to Rugby.*

36. Leicester Fowler 4P 2-6-4 tank No 42413 dashes down the grade near Churchover, between Ullesthorpe and Rugby, with the 4.20 pm from Leicester Midland to Rugby.

37. An interesting variation during steam's last years was the Cleethorpes-Birmingham through train which produced an Eastern Region B1 4-6-0 from Immingham shed for the round trip. Here No 61318 curves to join the Midland main line at Wigston North Junction on its way home from

38. A Stanier 3P 2-6-2 tank No 40138 belonging to Nuneaton shed calls at the former Wigston Glen Parva station with the 6.9pm local from Nuneaton Trent Valley to Leicester London Road.

39. Having run round its train, a Leicester Fowler 2-6-4 tank No 42331 pulls into the up platform at Nuneaton Abbey Street with the 1.10pm Saturday 'shoppers' train to Leicester London Road. The station is obviously an ideal venue for both professional and public gossip. April 1960.

LEICESTER

If the early years of my life were spent within sound of the Great Central at Leicester they were also spent within both sound and glimpse of the Midland branch to Coalville and Burton on Trent. Indeed, but for the row of tall, Edwardian houses on the opposite side of the road which effectively screened the railway I would have enjoyed far more than the neck-craning oblique 'snatch' available from our own attic windows. How often I wished that we could have changed sides of the road but the memory can nevertheless still furnish images of the 9.20am local passenger train from Leicester to Burton headed by a red Compound as it crossed the bridge over nearby Fosse Rd. South.

It was in 1937 that the topic of moving house began to creep into the domestic gossip of the Walker household and there was mention of a property with a railway at the bottom of the garden. The move took place in the winter of that year and my personal transfer was accomplished after that of the furniture, kitchen effects, laundry, garden tools and religious tracts by which time it was dark. In the best Victorian tradition I was rapidly despatched to bed so that I would be neither seen nor heard while some order was established on the ground floor.

My long, narrow bedroom was situated at the rear of the house and some newly machined curtains covered the windows. Sleep must have been about to cloud the consciousness when the sound of a train drifted into the remnants of wakefulness. At first it was distant but its volume steadily grew until its closeness was too immediate to be ignored and I dived out of bed to stumble down the room and snatch the curtains open. There, below, and only some 150 yards away, were the shapes of a goods train whose engine puffed and clanked its way past while the occupants of its footplate were both highlit or silhouetted by the glare from the fire. I had precious little sleep that night and when daylight came made a delighted re-acquaintance with the Leicester to Burton branch only this time it was in full view and beyond it was a goodly acreage of allotment gardens.

True, the novelty had to wear off but the pleasure of watching a remarkable variety of trains on that busy branch line never really palled and in those formative years, which included the tensions of the 2nd World war, it provided a sense of both continuity and warm security. Even during the darkest of blackouts I could lie in bed and identify every type of engine that passed simply by the sound of its exhaust and motion. If they passed during an air raid alert I also fervently hoped as I cowered beneath the sheets that the tarpaulins covering the gap between engine cab and tender were sufficiently effective to conceal the glow from the fire so that it would not be spotted by the German bombers.

Compound, 3P and 2P 4-4-0s; Fowler and Stanier 2-6-4 tanks; Stanier 3P 2-6-2 tanks; 'Crab' and Stanier 2-6-0s; Stanier 'Black fives' and the occasional 'Jubilee' and 'Patriot' 4-6-0 headed the branch passenger trains while the inevitable 4F,3F and 2F 0-6-0s; Stanier 8Fs and the odd, wayward ex L.N.W. 'Super D' 0-8-0 moved the coal from the pits in the Leicestershire coalfield throughout both day and night and 'Crabs' ran the beer from Burton.

The Burton branch did more than pass my home. Its intermittent sounds permeated the roads where my friends lived and they punctuated the games we played in the nearby park. The ringing side rods of the old Midland 2P and 3P 4-4-0s jogging past our homes in Dorchester Road, Ainsdale Road, Kingswood Avenue and Hinckley Road were a comforting audible background to our young lives and we all knew what type of engines they were without having to see them. The same indeed was true of the No 3 tramcars that terminated their journeys from Leicester's Clock Tower at Western Park. The sound and rhythm of their wheels on the tram line joints combined with the audible pitch of their electric motors identified their location very clearly. Their clattering familiarity and remarkable longevity somehow made for a slower and deeper sense of being and 'rootedness' that has now sadly gone.

The secondary school I attended in Leicester was to increase my contacts with things Midland and L.M.S. To reach the school meant a road crossing either above or below the main line south of the city's London Road station. Indeed, the shortest route to school actually accompanied the railway for several yards before crossing it close to the gates of the Victorian cemetery on the Welford Road.

This overcrowded municipal graveyard was part of an interesting square mile of Leicester which also included the school with its playing fields, the University College, the cattle market with its associated abattoirs and pungent fertiliser works and the historic Freeman's Common. On a warm Summer day when the funerary stonework had absorbed some heat the cemetery was a relaxing and quite benevolent place to squat or sprawl and watch the trains go by. The activity on the railway effectively countered any thoughts of mortality which rarely impinged on pre-adolescence anyway but if they did they were far more likely to be aroused by the scenes occasionally on offer on the other side of the railway. Here, the huddled and sometimes distressed occupants of the cattle vans in the Cattle Dock sidings were 'hollered', prodded and poked into pens before being driven into the abattoirs to meet their demise.

Alongside the cemetery wall was Cattle Market Sidings signal box. Besides controlling access and exit to and from the livestock sidings it also controlled the up and down fast and slow lines. The down slow line signals which were close to the box included a fixed distant arm and many freight trains whistled a code of a long and two shorts to the duty signalman to indicate whether or not they were to be routed into the reception line for the Leicester goods depot which was north of the station. The intention was then transmitted to his signal box colleagues down the line at London Rd. Junction, Leicester North and Bell Lane boxes.

In the southbound direction, after they had first passed beneath the main Welford Road girder bridge , the slow and fast lines parted and each burrowed separately beneath the Freeman's Common through the short Knighton tunnels. Freeman's Common was a fascinating reserve tenanted by selected freemen of the City of Leicester and was given over to allotment cultivation much of which had gone wild. Among the warren of footpaths and overgrown plots however were odd red-brick secretive houses and cottages often concealed by tall hedges and uncontrolled shrubs. It was a strange and curious wilderness and strictly out of bounds to young train spotters. They, of course, ignored the prohibition and invariably made their way to the south end of the tunnels where a wide grass-covered cutting afforded a relaxing cushion as well as an excellent view of both fast and slow lines. Furthermore,it also looked out across the triangle of the Knighton Junctions where the Burton branch diverged. Away from road traffic and people it was a delightful oasis where one could recline among the fescues and clovers to watch the movement and passing of trains both passenger and freight.Also, because of the concealing tunnels, there was always an element of surprise with up trains which added a certain spice.

It has to be said that the cattle market did not always offer sinister associations. Sometimes it could provide hilarious entertainment as when, on one memorable occasion queues of trains were held on each side of the Knighton tunnels while frantic attempts were made to recapture a well developed male specimen of a Lincolnshire large white pig. With a fine sense of independence it had made a bid for freedom from the cattle market lairage and escaped into the cover of the tunnel. As the garbled and muffled shouts of the drovers filtered out of the main line portal our porkine hero charged his assailants to give them the slip before running at a brisk trot back along the railway in the direction of London Road station. Whether he made it is not known but if he did then his appearance on Platform 2 would no doubt have added to the perplexity of those passengers waiting for the much delayed express from St. Pancras whose train was being held up somewhere near Wigston.

The Midland line was also briefly glimpsed from the school playing fields but trains were too distant to be thoroughly identified as they passed the south junction at Knighton. On the other hand there were school friends from the area who were resident in some extremely favourable spots. There was 'Wag' Spooner, for example, whose parents held the licence of the Manchester Hotel in Knighton Fields Road East which was solidly placed alongside the railway embankment and bridge close to Knighton South Junction. 'Wag' and I spent a number of carefree summer afternoons perched on the roof of one of the pub's outbuildings round the back with an excellent view of the passing traffic. A supply of suitable liquid refreshment and sandwiches was also provided.

Another school friend who lived half a mile from the line near Knighton village was able to provide comfortable chairs and a powerful pair of binoculars as compensation for the lack of immediacy when we occupied his upstairs landing. Some deft panning was practised through the window to catch the cabside numerals of engines as they distantly passed the gap between the two houses opposite.

In the 1940s passenger traffic over the Midland at Leicester was quite heavy and this was well illustrated during the evening rush hour between 4pm and 5pm. when a whole procession of trains departed from the south end of London Road station. The 4.8 to Nuneaton Trent Valley with its antique ex L.N.W. Webb 2-4-2 tank or Stanier 3P tank would be followed by a Fowler 4P 2-6-4 tank on the 4.14 to Rugby. Next there would be a Compound on the 4.40 to Birmingham ; a 2P or 3P 4-4-0 on the 4.45 pm to Burton on Trent and finally a Stanier 'Jubilee' on the 4.50 to St. Pancras.

Three miles south of Leicester were the three stations, junctions and another triangle at Wigston. Here at the north junction, the Midland main line parted company with the branches to Rugby and Birmingham and the historic sequence of the complex was interestingly clear with the original Midland Counties route of 1840 which joined up with the London and Birmingham line at Rugby taking an almost straight course through the station at South Wigston and on through Countesthorpe, Broughton Astley, Leire Halt and Ullesthorpe. The Midland main line which was constructed later in 1857 to connect with the Great Northern at Hitchin, curved strongly away to the left to pass through Wigston Magna station while curving away right at the North Junction and passing through Wigston Glen Parva station was the line to Nuneaton and Birmingham. This was originally a London & North Western branch from Nuneaton (South Leicestershire Railway) and was opened in 1864.

During and immediately after the 2nd World war both the former Midland and Great Central lines through Leicester were extremely busy but in spite of having the advantage of slow lines for its freight traffic the Midland often seemed to be cluttered and congested. This was partly due to the number of branches it 'collected' but the problem was also exacerbated by the arrangements at Wigston North Junction where the down slow line was transferred across both main lines to the up side to keep company with the up slow road.

Obstacles like this were not unusual on the Midland and when in addition short stretches of four track were reduced to two as between Wistow and Kilby bridge it was not surprising that freight trains consumed large chunks of time waiting to clear such impediments. A further complication awaited goods traffic destined for Leicester's goods depot at Queen Street. This was on the down side of the railway so that any traffic for Leicester goods yard had to be taken across the main lines which involved yet another messy manoeuvre.

For all its undoubted virtue as an architectural expression of the Railway Age at street level, Leicester London Road station was a gloomy and depressing environment down below on the platforms at least at the south end. However, as a junior, if one wanted to get close to engines without the risks of trespass it was the only legal opportunity available. The London expresses with their 'Jubilee' 5XPs were always relished and the even, three cylinder 'ticka-ticka-ticka' of their valve motion as they ran up and stopped in Platform 3 were particularly memorable. So too were their departures when the first open beats of their exhaust would suddenly be muffled by the overbridge beneath London Road through which they disappeared into a pungent cocktail of their own smoke and steam.

The north end of the platforms at Leicester London Road were out in the open and more pleasantly 'airy'. They pushed their ramps below another bridge carrying Swain Street and this long bridge stretched over the station sidings. platforms, tracks and goods lines. Up above at street level it was an unusual construction in that the pedestrian sidewalks were separated from the roadway by the lattice girder work of the bridge's superstructure. This sloped up from the road level onto four flat-topped steel 'seats' on each side of the road which overlooked the plate sides thus affording a good view down onto the railway particularly on the station side. However, it was an uncomfortable and decidedly unofficial vantage point because its rivetted surface was not exactly kind to the buttocks and also Swain Street was rather close to the city police headquarters. Indeed spotters who perched on its girder tops were actually visible from the police station windows and risked being spotted themselves.

In the 1940s Swain Street was still surfaced with granite sets which gave road vehicles a characteristic 'lumpy' sound as they climbed onto and crossed the bridge. Beyond the bridge they curved to pass that grim local institution Hillcrest Hospital which was really the 'Workhouse'. This was the setting of a rare and bizarre experience for the author. It was the afternoon of Friday, March 29th 1946 and he was sitting aloft on the bridge girders observing things L.M.S. It was 2.20 and his attention was abruptly distracted by a loud crunching sound. Turning, he watched incredulously as Leicester Corporation double decker bus No 286 of elderly Leyland Titan vintage bound for Coleman Road having collided with the workhouse wall began slowly to tip over onto its side with a dull, excruciating thud. The muffled screams and shouts of

shocked 'and injured passengers then followed before they began to crawl out of the narrow emergency door at the rear of the bus. Fortunately there were no fatalities but the episode certainly put paid to any further railway interest that day.

If the windows at the rear of Hillcrest Hospital tended to accumulate more of a patina than those at the front it was perhaps because they looked down upon Leicester's Midland engine shed- code No 15C. So too did the footpath which followed the outside of the Workhouse wall and by means of a right angle connected Swain Street with Hutchinson Street. As the path also looked down onto the shed yard it was protected by a heavy wire mesh fence which, like many such structures invited the obvious title of the 'birdcage'. Through the openings in its soot-covered weave many generations of train spotters and watchers observed the movements and manoeuvres down below and while the depot was not in the Premier division where express passenger engines were concerned it still presented an enormous variety as befitting an important railway crossroads. Just prior to nationalisation it was quite normal to find over 20 different locomotive types in and around the shed.

North of Leicester, its shed and goods depot the railway ran above the city streets and both slow lines were kept together on the up side of the fast tracks as they had done since Wigston North Junction. At Humberstone Road Junction the Midland crossed over that entertaining local institution the former G.N. Leicester Belgrave Road branch with its first world war connection which was later removed and then temporarily restored after the closure of the branch in 1964. Then, another four miles further on at Syston the Midland reached yet another junction triangle. Here, eastbound trains parted from the main line and headed for Melton Mowbray. This route is taken up in a separate essay.

A final, formative, teenage memory of things L.M.S. at Leicester was the office of Mr. Tandy. That gentleman was the local Commercial Manager after the war and his 'empire' was located in a busy office alongside the station in London Road. It may be difficult to believe now that.it was once possible at the age of 16 to enter the Commercial office and personally present oneself at the desk of one of his scores of clerks to request a shed permit for any depot on the L.M.S. Details would be taken and a week later after the shed had been approached and approval received the pad of official forms would be removed from the desk drawer and a permit made out in the name of the applicant. On arrival at the depot the foreman would provide a 'spare' man to act as 'legal' guide while the visit went ahead. A number of such permits still remain in the Walker personal archives.

When I took up serious photography in 1957 I was delighted to find that so many of the familiar locomotive 'characters' I had grown up with were still at work though for many of the older types their days were severely numbered. Only the war had ensured their survival. The expresses still gave employment to Stanier 'Jubilees' and Black 5s but despite their staged accelerations the Midland did seem to lack the cavalier flair that continued to imbue the Great Central section which even them was being considered for closure. At the time many Midland line expresses were resorting to double heading often with some distinctly dubious and antique 4-4-0 assistance in order to keep time.

Unlike the Great Central shed at Leicester the Midland depot had little to do with the running of the line's expresses which was more the responsibility of crews from London's Kentish Town, Derby, Nottingham, Sheffield Millhouses, Manchester Trafford Park, and Leeds Holbeck. Leicester's function was more bound up with local passenger, branch line and freight work of which there was plenty.

Midland expresses made no engine change at Leicester and their locomotives were usually well warmed up by the time they made their call at London Rd. station. Photographically their departures often lacked the visual energy offered by a fresh, 'cold' and moist engine. Instead one had to look to the keen temperatures of a winter day to capture some real visual action. Local trains were a different matter and often began their journeys visually 'fresh' and smokey.

It was good to be able to wander around the haunts of one's boyhood with official permission and actually 'get among' the trains at spots like Wigston Junction, Freeman's Common, London Road Junction and Humberstone Road. The resulting photographs bring back memories of happy, carefree days which were enriched by that machine of wonder and 'colour', the steam locomotive.

40. *Back on the main line a 'Black 5' No 44985 emerges from Knighton tunnel with the up 'Thames-Clyde Express'. Above the tunnel is Freeman's Common.*

41. *The grey morning of 30th July 1959 finds a Stanier Class 5 No 45139 hurrying past Knighton Junction with the 8.5 am express from Derby to St. Pancras.*

43 The Liverpool-Preston branch. An 8F No 48007 on its way out of Liverpool, with a mixed freight...

42 In the late evening of July 18th 1960 after a heavy shower 'Britannia' 'Pacific' No 70017...

45. *The fireman of No 40452 looks out for the guard's 'Right away' at Desford.*

44. *On an evening in high summer a Leicester 2P 4-4-0 No 40452 heading the 5.34 pm local train from Leicester London Road to Burton on Trent rolls in to Kirby Muxloe which was the first stop out of Leicester. 18.6.59.*

colliery sidings at Ellistown between Coalville and Desford on the Burton-Leicester line with an R.C.T.S./L.C.G.B. enthusiast special from Derby. In the background rises the mild granite prominence of Bardon Hill which at 900 feet is the highest hill in Leicestershire. 11.5.63

ine of 1832 which was one of our original railways. From Desford Junction this single track r'ell arrived in Leicester at the city's West Bridge terminus having passed through Groby, Ratby, Glenfield and Robert Stephenson's 1,796 yard Glenfield tunnel. It survived as a freight-only line until 1966 carrying coal into Leicester from the local coalfield and providing an exit for stone from the granite quarries at Ratby and Groby. Because of space limitations inside Glenfield tunnel the motive power was restricted to the Midland 2F 0-6-0s until the last years when some of the small Ivatt 2MT 2-6-0s were adapted to work over the line. In this picture a 2F 0-6-0 No 58137 with the larger cab shunts at Groby and collects some loaded wagons from the local granite quarry.

Keene were a happy and cheerful duo with few professional worries on a line like the Leicester West Bridge branch. There were, however, always the hazards arising from juvenile activities in the mile-long Glenfield tunnel.

station with the afternoon empties from Leicester West Bridge to Coalville. Because of the proximity of the *New Parks* housing estate with its high juvenile population it became the custom to travel through the historic bore with some caution to give any young high-risk trespassers and adventurers time to vacate the tunnel ahead of the approaching train!

50. *The Glenfield gateman walks up to open the crossing gates and allow No 58137 to proceed on its way with the afternoon freight from Leicester West Bridge to Coalville. The original crossing keeper's cottage is visible on the right.*

51. *Back on the main Leicester- Burton branch a 4F 0-6-0 No 43979 sets off from Desford with the 5.34pm local train from Leicester London Rd. to Burton. 22.7.60*

53. *At the other end a Standard Class 5 No 73141 hurries out of Knighton Tunnel on its way into Leicester with the 6.10 pm from Birmingham New St.*

Previous Page
52. *A 'Jubilee' No 45631 'Tanganyika' makes a fine sight as she bursts out of Knighton Tunnel with the 10.20 am cup final special from Leicester London Road to Wembley Hill. 'Tanganyika' was the first 'Jubilee' I ever saw when I was a small boy. It was then a red engine and brand new. Interestingly the setting was a cutting between Knighton and Wigston Junctions only a mile or so beyond this spot. 25.5.63.*

54. *A photograph out of the fireman's cab window finds Stanier 'Jubilee' No 45590 'Travancore' looking rather neglected and unkempt heading out of Leicester and approaching Cattle Market sidings with the 7.0am express from Sheffield to St. Pancras. 1.8.59.*

55. The up 'Thames-Clyde Express' again running late with Class 5 No 44853 is given an assistant engine of the same type. No 44811 from the local depot at Leicester for the journey on to St.

56. *Wembley Cup Final Special. Rattles and streamers are already in evidence in the carriage windows as Jubilee No 45585 'Hyderabad' gathers speed near Cattle Market sidings with a train for Wembley Hill. 25.5.63*

Following Page
57. *Passing beneath the Regent Road overbridge 'Jubilee' No 45585 'Hyderabad' again makes a dignified departure from Leicester with the up 'Palatine'.*

58. *Another cup final special bound for Wembley Hill sets off from Leicester London Road and passes between the... retaining walls of New Walk cutting headed by 'Jubilee' No.45649...*

59. *A Stanier 'Jubilee' No 45628 'Somaliland' coasts into Leicester through the New Walk cutting with the 10.25 am from St. Pancras to Manchester Central.*

60. As the expresses on the Western Division of the London Midland Region were steadily turned over to diesel haulage so some of its larger steam types became available for transfer to Midland services and depots. Here a 'Royal Scot' No 46152 'The Kings Dragoon Guardsman' formerly belonging to Crewe North and now briefly transferred to Kentish Town depot passes through the New Walk cutting on its way out of Leicester with the 10.25 hrs from Manchester Central to St

61. A photograph taken from the other side of the New Walk cutting catches Nottingham Stanier Class 5 No 44658 heading south with the 2.5 pm local from Leicester London Rd to

Previous Page 62. *A nicely turned out 'Jubilee', No 45610 'Gold Coast', pulls away from Leicester London Road and through the New Walk cutting with the 10.25 am express from Manchester Central to St. Pancras.*

63. *A shot from the New Walk overbridge catches Class 5 No 45277 accelerating away with the up 'Thames-Clyde Express' after the Leicester stop. Travelling towards the station a Fowler 4P tank heads a local from Rugby.*

64. *On 14th October 1962 The Locomotive Club of Great Britain ran a special train from London to Derby and back travelling out by the Great Central and back by the Midland route. The return run utilised one of the last of the unrebuilt 'Patriot' 4-6-0s No 45543 'Home Guard' which was 'borrowed' from Carnforth depot. By the time the return special arrived at Leicester London Road station on a grey evening the daylight had faded to such an extent that I had to get as close to the station as I could so that the combination of a slow engine speed, slow shutter speed and a fast film might capture something worthwhile. This was the result.*

65. I have to confess that I took very few photographs on Leicester's Midland station partly because I found it a somewhat dreary environment and perhaps because I preferred more solitary locations and settings where I could concentrate without distraction. This exception caught an unusual combination with a Crewe 'Jubilee' No. 45674 *Duncan* attached to a BR Standard Stanier Stanier 2P 2-6-2 tank No. 40157. The...

66. A shot inside the roundhouse at Leicester Midland shed finds a Fairburn 4P tank ...

67. One of three long exposure photographs taken during the dark hours at Leicester Midland shed when 'Royal Scot' No 46115 'Scots Guardsman' was a notable visitor to the roundhouse.

68. Another nocturnal experiment at Leicester Midland shed that was intended to include some lunar illumination which alas was obscured by cloud just as the exposure began. The engine was 4F No 44034. Strange things are said to happen at the time of the full moon!

Following Pages.
69. A bright but hazy morning finds 'Jubilee' No 45654 'Hood' pulling out of Leicester Midland and passing the engine shed with the down 'Thames-Clyde Express'.

70. A Saltley 'Crab' 2-6-0, No 42764 has just returned from a 'shopping' judging from its smart condition. It is seen heading out of Leicester and approaching Humberstone Road Station with the 10.18 am Summer Saturday train from Birmingham New Street to Yarmouth Vauxhall.

... out against a light under ... Junction with the up 'Thames-Clyde Express'. June 1960

... out of Leicester and approaching Humberstone Road station with the 12.55 pm train to Peterborough. 2.1.62.

75. *Double Takes. Approaching Humberstone Road Junction a 2P 4-4-0 No 40493 heading the*

76. *A 'Jubilee' No 45712 'Victory' dashes past Humberstone Road with the 7.25 am express from*

Previous Page.
77. *A Christmas Eve relief to the down 'Thames-Clyde Express' accelerates away from Leicester near Humberstone Road Junction signal box headed by Jubilee' No 45628 'Somaliland'. 24.12.1959*

78. *On the up slow line approaching Humberstone Road Junction a 'Crab' 2-6-0 No 42928 makes slow progress into Leicester with another train load of coal from the Nottinghamshire pits.*

79. *A 'Jubilee' 4-6-0 No 45592 'Barbados' pulls out of Loughborough Midland and past the Brush works with the 4.25 pm from St. Pancras to Derby. July 1961.*

MIDLAND LINES IN THE EAST MIDLANDS

On some recent journeys between Leicester and Nottingham by the Midland route not a single freight train was to be seen on the slow lines in either direction during the whole run. How different things were in the 1950s and early 60s when train loads of coal closely followed one another having been despatched from Toton yard at short intervals. Their 9Fs, 8Fs, 'Crabs', 'Austerities' and 4Fs would amble south to Syston Junction balanced by trains of returning empties.

At Syston most would leave the main line which continued into Leicester and instead they would turn eastward along the 1846 branch to Peterborough. This utilised the placid Wreake valley to Melton Mowbray. Here, their route would be joined from the north by the Midland's main line from Nottingham which had made its journey through the tunnels, cuttings and over the generous embankments of the Leicestershire/Nottinghamshire border wolds.

Continuing eastwards from Melton trains then kept company with the River Eye to skirt Stapleford Park.At Saxby Junction where the single line connecting with the M.& G.N. continued its way eastwards, Midland trains curved south again to enter that diminutive rural gem of a county, Rutland. Then, running along Catmose Vale the railway passed through Oakham where the town's level crossings provided a somewhat false reading of the landscape to come because south of the county town the line ran into conflict with the grain of the country. From now on the rolling marlstone uplands demanded a sequence of tunnels and changes of gradient. The first tunnel at Manton was driven through the high ground separating the Rivers Gwash and Chater and at the junction station the original Midland line to Stamford and Peterborough turned away eastwards. A considerable amount of freight took this route on its way to the South East of England via the marshalling yard at Whitemoor. The Midland main line however, continued south at Manton onto its most stylish section. This included three more tunnels in fairly rapid succession and the last of them at Seaton ushered trains into an impressive crossing of the Welland Valley.

To carry its railway across this spacious valley the Midland had to construct a viaduct stretching for 1275 yards consisting of 82 arches each with a 40 foot span and where it crossed over the river it did so at a height of 60 feet. When built in the late 1870s it consumed 15 million bricks. Local clay deposits were used and the bricks were kilned 'on site' but they proved to be inferior and weathered badly. As they crumbled and fell they had to be replaced by engineers blue bricks of more robust strength and density. Happily, though the through route to Nottingham has gone, the viaduct and the railway it carries is still with us and like the Forth bridge with its constant need for paint its restoration and brick replacement continues as an ongoing activity. Rarely is the viaduct without some scaffolding.

For southbound trains the viaduct marked the commencement of a six mile climb mostly at 1 in 200 as they transferred from the surging hills of the marlstone country on the Rutland side of the Welland to the equally surging hills of the limestone country of upland Northamptonshire into which county the line now ran. This was the country of the draglines, those enormous excavators that ponderously 'walked' themselves around the ironstone workings on the heights stripping the overburden with their long jibs before depositing it on the spoil tips . The ironstone was then exposed ready for mechanical shovel removal and despatch to the furnaces at nearby Corby and to other steel making centres. The distant draglines were an essential part of the landscape and emphasised the thoroughly indigenous character of steel making at Corby, a proud local industry that has now been eliminated as has the older, more historic works at Holwell near Asfordby where the Midland main line from Nottingham descended into Melton Mowbray.

Spring afternoons and Summer evenings spent in the Welland Valley with a camera are remembered with acute pleasure. Looking out from the airy heights around Seaton with the stone villages of Harringworth, Gretton, Wakerley, Barrowden, Tixover and distant Duddington all marked by their church spires or towers one was presented with an area of English pastoral landscape at its best. Below, the organic rhythm of the viaduct arches crossed the scene and in a Westering sun its brickwork glowed with a wonderful, subdued warmth. As with so many railway structures that were built with sympathetic materials and were designed to respect and compliment their setting the viaduct stood as a man-made enhancement to an already attractive landscape.

Something of the historic sequence of railways in this gentle valley was fascinatingly evident from a visual study of the network of lines using it. Built firmly on the valley floor was the first line on the scene which was the 1851 L.N.W.R route from Rugby and Market Harborough which ran to a junction with the Midland's Peterborough line at Luffenham. This was followed in 1879 by the same company's Seaton-Wansford link. By traversing the woodland country around Westhay and Fineshade which separates the Welland and Nene valleys it was able to join its Northampton to Peterborough line at Yarwell Junction near Wansford. Then, late in the day in 1894,the L.N.W. also constructed a short branch from its Luffenham line up to the town of Uppingham.

It is doubtful if the opening of any of these lines and their sleepy train services did much to disturb the bucolic peace of the Welland Valley around the Junction at Seaton and its neighbouring village of Harringworth. Passenger trains to and from Market Harborough, Peterborough, Luffenham and Uppingham appeared on the scene almost discreetly and seemed to want to linger in the landscape. In the best branch line tradition their station stops were leisurely and thoroughly befitted an unruffled pace of life that perhaps belonged to another age.

In contrast Midland line trains treated the valley with scant regard. Harringworth viaduct, though constructed on a gradient rising towards the south, nevertheless marked the bottom of a long dip for trains in both directions. The appearance and passage of expresses was both fast and fleeting while even the freight trains seemed to waste little time crossing the valley. Northbound trains visibly announced their approach quite early as having passed Gretton village, they made a distant,curving descent eastward with the valley for a good mile and a half before turning north again through Harringworth station to rush the viaduct crossing. In the opposite direction London bound expresses having enjoyed the benefit of a three mile descent mostly at 1 in 167 offered no such warning as they burst out of Seaton tunnel to bound over the arches bridging the two low level lines and then the 82 of the long viaduct. There was never any doubt about the Midland's main line status!

80. *A 'Royal Scot' No 46160 'Queen Victoria's Rifleman' dashes out of Asfordby tunnel on Nottingham-Melton main line with the 8.52 am express from Bradford Forster Square to S Pancras. In the background the chimneys of Holwell ironworks are active. 1.7.61.*

81. At Melton Junction a Fairburn 2-6-4 tank No 42184 takes the Nottingham line with the Nottingham and Derby portion of

82. A Nuneaton 'Patriot' 4-6-0 No 45537 'Private E. Sykes V.C.' heads out of Melton Mowbray with the 3.45 pm from Peterborough to Leicester London Road. 1.7.61.

Following Page.
83. After being delayed at Melton Junction a Stanier 8F 2-8-0 No 48303 puts up an impressive exhaust as it approaches the town with an up coal train.

84. A Colwick B1 No 61141 sets off from Melton Mowbray

85. In Rutland's marlstone country an 8F No 48547 from

86. *Another 8F No 48704 heads south through the rolling uplands between Glendon and Seaton tunnels with a train of lime for Corby steel works. August*

87. A shot from the Midland line above sees a Standard 4 4-6-0 No 75055 drifting quietly towards Seaton Junction with an evening freight from Luffenham. The line from Peterborough can be seen converging from the left. 28.6.62.

Following Pages.
88. A Standard Class 5 4-6-0 No 73139 dashes out of Seaton tunnel and approaches the Welland valley crossing with the 1.57 pm express from Sheffield to St. Pancras.

89. On an afternoon of Spring sunshine a 'Black 5' No 45277 hurries over the arches of Harringworth viaduct with a St. Pancras-Bradford express.

Previous Page.
90. Stanier 'Jubilee' No 45579 'Punjab' heads towards Seaton tunnel after crossing the Welland valley with the 2.15 pm

91. Having crossed Harringworth viaduct and the line to Peterborough an 8F 2-8-0 No 48386 approaches the bridge over the Luffenham and Uppingham lines as it heads north with a down train of empties. On the skyline considerable interest is attracting ... ...

92. Crossing the 82 arch viaduct in the southbound direction a 9F heads an up coal train. Harringworth village and its parish church of St. John the Baptist catches the evening sunlight while in the foreground are the signals controlling the low level junction at Seaton. Also conspicuous is the fire gutted roof of ...

93. *Making tracks for Peterborough from Seaton Junction a Stanier 'Black 5' heading the 5.23pm from Rugby is about to pass beneath the Midland main line. 28.6.62.*

94. *On an afternoon in March 1963 a Stanier 8F No 48608 from Royston depot in Yorkshire hurries across Harringworth viaduct with a train of iron ore bound for South Yorkshire.*

Trent Junction

95. Hurrying out of the castellated portal of Red Hill tunnel on the approach to Trent Junction is 'Jubilee' No 45622 'Nyasaland' with a relief to the down 'Thames-Clyde Express'.
26.3.59.

96. The Midland's crossing of the River Trent at Trent Junction involved separate bridges for fast and slow lines. Here, a 'Britannia' Pacific No 70017 'Arrow' crosses the river with an Easter extra from Manchester Central to St. Pancras.
26.3.59.

97. *A Carlisle Kingmoor 'Black 5' No 45083 fitted with a snowplough heads an up ballast train across the River Trent on the up main line. On the left of the picture the River Soar can be seen flowing in from Leicester and Loughborough while the bridge on the other bank of the Trent gives access to the Erewash Canal. 26.3.59.*

98. *A Wellingborough 9F 2-10-0 No 92018 heads north near Trent station along the goods line from Toton with an up coal train.*

Following Page.
99. *The double heading era. An elderly Midland 2P 4-4-0 No 40511 from Saltley depot in Birmingham finds itself assisting 'Black 5' No 44663 on the 12.15pm from St. Pancras to Bradford Forster Square. The pair are seen leaving Trent Junction.*
26.3.59.

100. *The experiment with the Franco-Crosti boiler on some of the 9F 2-10-0s was not exactly a success as this photograph shows. No 92022 is crossing the Trent with an up coal train from Toton yard and its exhaust is obviously obliterating the view ahead of the driver. The nightmare reputation they had with engine crews was well justified. 26.3.59.*

101. *Apart from some token black paint on its smoke box, Kentish Town 'Jubilee' No 45616 'Malta G.C.' looks to be in a sorry condition as it coasts into Trent Junction with the 12 noon semi-fast from Nottingham Midland to St. Pancras. 26.3.59.*

THE MIDLAND IN THE PEAK

It seems a little ironic that a railway company which became notorious for its policy of building lots of small engines and then rapidly resorting to double heading when loads threatened to overwhelm them should have engineered some of our most ambitious and demanding routes. It also absorbed and operated others like the Birmingham and Gloucester with its Lickey 'lift' and the energy-sapping Somerset and Dorset.

The Midland's main line to Manchester through the Peak District of Derbyshire was a bold and impressive venture. It continued an earlier line that the company had constructed from a junction at Ambergate through Matlock to Rowsley. Its onward extension over the Peak first to Buxton and then to Manchester entailed some heavy and heroic engineering, demanding gradients and, for locomotives, hard work.

It was towards the end of the war that I was taken on a journey from Leicester to Liverpool to visit some 'Scouse' relations scattered on both sides of the Mersey. I was 14 years old at the time and recall taking the Midland route to Manchester Central from where we caught a train into Liverpool Central. Details of the journey are now rather vague but I do remember the irritation of sitting with my back to the engine in a crowded compartment and on the 'wrong' side of the carriage so that the freight-filled slow lines and the engine sheds at Leicester and Derby were on the corridor side and effectively screened by standing passengers.

I also remember how soon after leaving Derby the line changed its character and what had been a brisk progress through the open landscape of the Soar and Trent valleys developed into a dour and demanding struggle. It was accompanied with some inspiring 3 cylinder 'Jubilee Music' from the front of the train as our engine toiled away through some increasingly massive terrain with bridges and viaducts over fast flowing rivers and tunnels beneath impressive heights. The scenery and sounds from the engine were, of course, inseparable and it was only when my interest in railways matured that I discovered that for almost 30 miles beyond Derby trains for Manchester had to tackle an almost continuous climb into the Peak District with very few 'breathers' until they reached a summit at Peak Forest and descended into the long and ominously named Dove Holes Tunnel.

The concentration of photographs within the short stretch between Great Longstone and Monsal Dale perhaps conveys something of the remarkably sudden changes that can occur in mountain limestone country often with little warning.

Apart from Haddon tunnel (which was driven not to overcome a natural obstacle but to conceal the railway from the Duke of Rutland's nearby stately home at Haddon Hall), there was little to prepare the passenger for the shock of emerging from Headstone tunnel into Monsal Dale. The climb to the tunnel was made in the open with a train conspicuous and even confidently in command of its setting. The transformation that awaited its entry into Monsal Dale was quite breathtaking and in such a massive landscape it became instead a diminutive thread of movement as it crossed 72 feet above the River Wye and ran along a ledge beside a stone reinforced wall to the next tunnel at Cressbrook.

I left it rather late to photograph steam in the Peak. The expresses were already diesel hauled and the line's closure was not far ahead. However, the flow of freight remained considerable and it was still steam hauled and banked. 8Fs, 9Fs and Black 5s were plentiful while to ensure the contempt provoked by familiarity there were still the inevitable 4F 0-6-0s plodding wearily through the hills. Perhaps such a landscape deserved better!

The climb into the Peak.
102. An 8F hurries north over the River Wye at Cromford with a down coal train. 1.8.64.

103. *The folly of Riber Castle dominates the skyline at Matlock as 8F 2-8-0 No 48318 hustles north through the station with a train of bogie bolsters.*

Following Page.
104. *Longstone station is closed but still in possession of its period lamps. A 4F 0-6-0 No 44421 climbs through the station with a mixed freight. 23.6.64.*

105. A Stanier Class 5 4-6-0 No 45329 is given rear end assistance as it climbs into the Peak district towards Headstone tunnel with a Corby- Glazebrook

106. A 9F No 92159 also with banker support climbs towards Headstone tunnel with a northbound

107. After passing through Headstone tunnel a Stanier Class 5 4-6-0 No 44780 with steam to spare enters Monsal Dale with a down coal train. 23.6.64

108. A prospect of Monsal Dale and the River Wye includes the sight of Fairburn 4P tank giving banking assistance to a northbound coal train. On

109. Another 9F 2-10-0 No 92018 hurries along Monsal Dale towards Cressbrook tunnel with a northbound train of fitted vans. 23.6.64.

110. Ambergate Junction. Approaching the short Toadmoor tunnel on the line to Clay Cross is Stanier Class 5 4-6-0 No 44919 with an express for Sheffield and York.

Following Page.
Chesterfield.
111. A photograph taken from the massive viaduct that once carried the former Lancashire, Derbyshire and East Coast line from its station at Chesterfield Market Place over both the Midland main line to Sheffield and the Great Central's Chesterfield loop at different levels. A Stanier 'Black 5' No 44919 with steam to spare hurries into Chesterfield with a northbound express. 29.7.61.

114. A 4F No 44122 plods slowly along the up slow line from Hull to
Birmingham. Dominating the skyline is the famous crooked spire of St.
Mary's and All Saints parish church. 29.7.61.

off from Chesterfield Midland with the 8.25 am
Bridge signal box at Chesterfield with a long train of iron ore tipplers.
29.7.61.

over the Great Central line and approaches the remains of the L.D. &
E.C. with an express for the West of England. 29.7.61.

The climb out of Sheffield.
115. *Local trains and 'Jubilees': The 2.23 pm local train from Sheffield Midland to Chinley is seen climbing the long 1 in 100 between Millhouses and Beauchief headed by No 45656 'Cochrane'. 29.7.61.*

116. *Passing Millhouses engine shed with the 2.58 pm Saturday stopping train from Sheffield to Derby is Derby's 'Jubilee' No 45627 'Sierra Leone'. 29.7.61.*

Following Page.
Birmingham
117. *Birmingham New Street station provided a showcase for some of the last remnants of the Midland Railway 4-4-0s before their withdrawal and scrapping. Here a 2P 4-4-0 No 40489 from Gloucester shed stands in Platform 7 after arriving with the 6.52 am from Gloucester Eastgate.*

118. An unrebuilt 'Patriot' No 45506 'The Royal Pioneer Corps' calls at Burton on Trent with the 7.40 am express from Bristol Temple Meads to Bradford. This innocent-looking photograph conceals a somewhat hair-raising episode. Earlier I had negotiated a footplate trip on the engine from Birmingham New Street to Burton with the Saltley crew in charge. As this took me a short distance beyond the limit of my Holiday Runabout Ticket it was my intention to return into the 'safety' of the ticket as quickly as possible after reaching Burton.

Alas, in my enthusiasm for a platform shot I forgot to collect my jacket from the hook inside the engine's cab where it had hung during the run. It was spotted just in time by the crew who hurriedly handed it to me as they pulled out with their train. But, as they did so the distant figure of the local station policeman was spotted. "Hey, watch that Copper", said Harold Bunt as No 45506 moved past with the train but his cautionary words were of no avail. I had been seen!

An interrogation followed in the station police office during which an appeal was made not to report the engine crew. My Runabout ticket was inspected and the modest excess fare preferred. A brief period of tense silence then ensued which ended with the words, "Don't worry, I shan't say anything. It's the real rogues we're after- not chaps like you". I returned to Birmingham on the next train not only greatly relieved but also with a distinctly more cordial view of the railway constabulary than I had perhaps held before. 29.7.59.

119. Another shot of 'Patriot' No 45506 'Royal Pioneer Corps' heading the 7.40 am express from Bristol Temple Meads to Bradford Forster Square. It is seen accelerating after a signal check near Wilnecote. 29.7.59.

120. '*Jubilee*' *No 45709* '*Implacable*' *stands in Platform 7 at New Street with an excursion to*

121. *On a murky morning another* '*Jubilee*' *No 45683* '*Hogue*' *waits in platform 7 with the 7.40am*

Temple Meads to Newcastle 1.8.60.

5 No 45265. 15.4.61

124. Five Ways was the first station on the way out of Birmingham on the main line to Bristol and it marked the last of the tunnels. For many years the station was closed and in a derelict condition. Here, a 'Jubilee' No 45662 'Kempenfelt' heads a relief to the 7.36 am from Sunderland to Bristol up the 1 in 80 gradient on 6th August 1960.

125. From the down platform at Five Ways another 'Jubilee' No 45602 'British Honduras' from Sheffield Millhouses depot climbs through with the 8.0am from Newcastle to Cardiff. 6.8.60

Following Page.
126. A Gloucester 'Crab' 2-6-0 No 42770 climbs past Five Ways with the 12.15 local train from Birmingham New Street to Worcester Shrub Hill. 6.8.60.

127. This was one of a number of photographs I obtained from the roof walks and fire escapes at Wrights rope making factory which was conveniently situated where the Midland lines rose up to the level of the Western Division lines at Grand Junction ready for the entry into New

128. A shot looking the other way of 4F 0-6-0 No 44580 coasting down the grade with a train of vans from Cadburys at Bournville. It is about to dive

129. A 'Black 5' No 45447 drifts down the grade and prepares to pass beneath ...the Western Division main line...

130. Photographed from the Western Division main line a Standard Class 5 No

Previous Page.

131. From a higher level on the roof of Wrights Ropes a 'Jubilee' 4-6-0 No. 45562 'Alberta' descends the grade ready to pass beneath the Western Division main line with the northbound 'Devonian'. The

132. A familiar and oft repeated sight at Landor Street Junction where a southbound freight consisting of empty car flats having collected a banker restarts its journey up the climb to Camp Hill. The train engine is 4F No. 44226, 20.8.62.

133. Two-way traffic at Brickyard Crossing where a Fowler 4P 2-6-4 tank No. 42417 gives vigorous banking assistance to a Class 5 which is heading a southbound freight up the gradient to Camp Hill. In the other direction a 4F No. 43963 reaches the bottom of the bank with a train of

Previous Page.
134. *Beginning the worst part of the climb to Camp Hill at 1 in 62 a 'Black 5' No 44810 crosses the Birmingham and Warwick Junction Canal and passes Brickyard Crossing signal box with a southbound freight. 19.8.63.*

135. *A 4F 0-6-0 No 44047 makes a typically smokey climb past Brickyard crossing box with a train of empties. 21.8.62.*

136. *A massive effort by Saltley 9F No 92157 climbing the 1 in 62 between Brickyard Crossing and St. Andrews Junction with a southbound coal train. 19.8.63.*

137. *In drenching rain another 9F No 92085 with a southbound coal train is in desperate trouble as it nearly slips to a standstill on the crossover at St Andrews*

The Lickey Incline
138. *Blackwell. Assisted in the rear by a single Western 84xx 0-6-0 Pannier tank, an 8F No 48315 reaches the top of the climb from Bromsgrove with a northbound train of vans and a cattle truck. Judging from the minimal banking support they would appear to be empty. 5.8.60.*

Following Pages.
139. *A Standard Class 5 4-6-0 No 73002 heading the 7.30 am from Newcastle to Bristol down the climb from Bromsgrove with a Standard Class 4 4-6-0 No 75022 which is on the way up with the 11.30 am from Gloucester Eastgate to Birmingham. 29.7.59.*

140. *On the climb is 'Crab' 2-6-0 No 42857 with the 1.48 pm from Gloucester to Birmingham. 29.7.59.*

142. *Half way up. A Stanier Class 5 No 44813 heading the 8.40 am from Bristol Temple Meads to Newcastle is also banked by a Western 84xx 0-6-0 Pannier Tank. 5.8.60.*

Previous Page.
141. *An original 'Patriot' 4-6-0 No 45506 'The Royal Pioneer Corps' makes a fine sight as it climbs serenely into the Lickey Hills with the 10.20 am relief express from Bristol to Sheffield.*

143. A 'Jubilee' No 45682 'Trafalgar' makes steady progress up the 1 in 37 with the 10.30 am express from Bristol to Newcastle. 5.8.60.

Following Page.

144. On the 10th of April 1961 it rained on Bromsgrove - heavily. While waiting for a lift into Wales I spent an hour or two on and around the station hoping the water would not penetrate my camera. Here in the continuous heavy downpour a Stanier 'Jubilee' No 45557 'New Brunswick' having collected some banking assistance sets off through Bromsgrove station with the 10.30 am express from Bristol Temple Meads to Newcastle. 10.4.61.

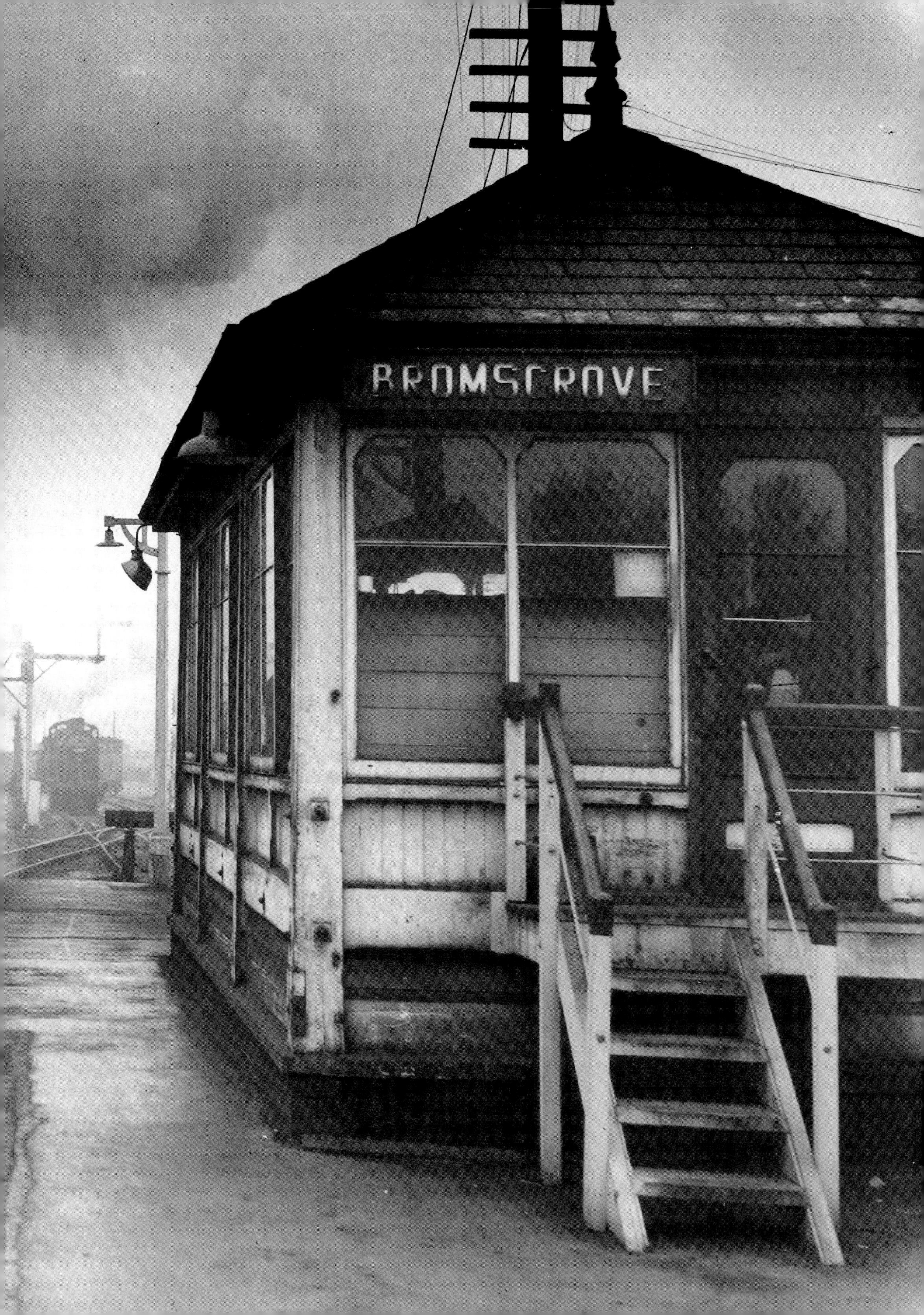
BROMSGROVE

146. *Under cloudy skies a Standard 4 4-6-0 No 75004 sets out from Bromsgrove with the 11.30 am from Gloucester to Birmingham New Street. 10.4.61.*

Bromsgrove with a northbound freight which is obviously bound for the breweries at Burton on Trent. 5.8.60.

148. *Worcester. A Stanier 'Black 5' No 44828 stands in Shrub Hill station with the 12.10 pm from Paignton to Bradford.*

Bristol Temple Meads to Sheffield while the fireman looks out to check that the bankers are in active support. Up on the footbridge a group of lads brave the rain in order to enjoy the pleasure of a momentary smoke screen. 10.4.61.

149. The starting signal at the north end of Worcester's Shrub Hill station is pulled off for 'Jubilee' No 45562 'Alberta' which is hauling the 4.25 pm to Derby. 3.8.60.

150. Gloucester. Another 'Jubilee' No 45570 'New Zealand' drifts past the engine shed and into Gloucester Eastgate with the 12.20 pm from Worcester Shrub Hill to Gloucester. 7.7.61.

Following Page.
151. The northbound 'Pines Express' is provided with some honoured motive power in the shape of No 46100 'Royal Scot'. It is seen leaving Gloucester Eastgate on 7th July 1961.

152. A 'Royal Scot' 4-6-0 No 46118 'Royal Welch Fusilier' stands at the buffer stops in Green Park station after arriving with the down 'Pines Express'. 7.7.61.

No 7307 ... double head the down 'Pines Express' out of ... Bath and engage in a ... these engines have a 1 in 50 climb ahead of them for nearly two miles they are making remarkably little fuss when it comes to smoke emission. 7.7.61.

154. *An S&D 2-8-0 No 53804 pulls out of Bath and passes the Junction signal box bound for Westerleigh sidings on the Bristol- Birmingham main line with a train of Somerset coal. 17.2.61.*

155. *Bath Junction signal box interior.*

158. No 53808 was the last S&D 2-8-0 to receive a shopping at Derby in May 1962. Here she is soon after her return to traffic making a fine climb of the 1 in 50 out of Bath past the site of the old brickworks near Claude Avenue with the 2 pm freight from Bath to Evercreech Junction. July 1962.

Class 4 No 75004 and 9F No 92245 seen near Claude Avenue coasting down the 1 in 50 from Combe Down into Bath. July 1962.

down the gradient and curves to pass Bath Junction box on its way into Bath with 2P 4-4-0 No 40569 and Standard 5 4-6-0 No 73050 providing the motive power. 17.2.61.

159. *A double chimney Standard 4 4-6-0 No 75071 makes a solo climb up the 1 in 50 to Combe Down with the 1.10 pm local train from Bath to Templecombe*

160. As his engine approaches the Claude Avenue overbridge, Bath driver George Hobbis snatches a glance back at the camera. His 4F, No 44558, is banking the 2 pm freight from Bath to Evercreech Junction up the 1 in 50 to Combe Down. 27.4.62.

Following Page.
161. Another S&D 2-8-0 No 53806 makes a fine curving climb up the 1 in 50 out of Bath behind the houses in West Avenue and Cynthia Rd. with the 2 pm goods to Evercreech Junction. 27.4.62.

162. *No 53810 again this time making a fine climb out of Devonshire tunnel and through the lovely Lyncombe Vale on the way up to Combe Down with the 11 am freight from Bath to Evercreech Junction.*

163. *A 2P 4-4-0 No 40700 drifts out of the south end of Combe Down tunnel with the 1.10 pm local from Bath Green Park to Bournemouth. The 1829 yard tunnel was notorious not only for its tight clearances but also for the fact that it possessed no ventilation shafts. On a day of busy traffic its passage could be very grim indeed for engine crews. 16.6.61.*

164. *On a grey winter afternoon in February 1962 S&D 2-8-0 No 53801 rushes the climb to Combe Down tunnel from the south with a train mainly of Somerset coal.*

165. *In somewhat different weather another S&D 2-8-0 No 53807 works coal empties tender first on the 12.35 pm train from Bath to Radstock and Norton Hill collieries. The train is free wheeling round the curve from Tucking Mill viaduct and skirting the grounds of Midford Castle. 16.6.61*

166. A Standard Class 4 4-6-0 No 75071 hurries towards the south end of Combe Down tunnel with the 12 noon train from Templecombe to Bath 16.6.61

167. In its last years the 2pm goods from Bath to Evercreech Junction often had no load to take and therefore travelled out engine and brake van to collect a train. Here on a dull winter afternoon in February 1962

168. *Rushing the climb in the other direction 2P No 40569 and Standard Class 5 No 73067 hustle the up 'Pines Express' over the viaduct and towards Combe Down tunnel and Bath. 16.6.61.*

169. *A Standard Class 4 4-6-0 No 75002 hurries away from Tucking Mill viaduct with the 9.53 am from Bath Green Park to Bournemouth. 27.4.62.*

Previous Page.
170. Skirting the grounds of Midford Castle Standard Class 4 4-6-0 No 75023 and Standard Class 5 4-6-0 No 73054 rush the climb to Combe Down tunnel with the up 'Pines Express'.
27.4.62.

171. With its tablet catcher conspicuously evident a 4F No 44146 dashes over Midford viaduct with a mixed freight bound for Bath.

172. The days of the S&D 2-8-0s were over when I obtained this shot of 8F No 48737 which has all its sanders working to assist it in its climb from Midford to Combe Down tunnel with a coal train from Radstock. 27.4.62.

173. On a dull, 'heavy' day in June 1961 the original 9F 2-10-0 No 92000 approaches the summit of the climb to Masbury from the north with the 7.35 am from Nottingham to

174. From the other side of the line on the same day a 2P 4-4-0 No 40569 running light is seen hurrying back from Bath to Evercreech Junction in order to pilot another northbound train over

175. *Driver Albert Selman at the regulator of S&D 2-8-0 No 53809 en route to Evercreech Junction with the 2 pm goods from Bath. 17.2.61.*

176. *A shot from the cab of S&D 2-8-0 No 53809 working the 2 pm goods from Bath to Evercreech Junction. Approaching Radstock. 17.2.61*

178. *Albert Selman provides another study in occupational discomfort as he studies the line ahead from the cab of S&D 2-8-0 No 53809 which is working the 2 pm goods from Bath to Evercreech Junction. 17.2.61.*

Following Page.
179. *With the load now reduced to a brake van S&D 2-8-0 No 53809 pauses in the mist at Shepton Mallet for water before beginning the descent to Evercreech Junction. 17.2.61.*

177. *No 53809 climbs into a Mendip mist near Chilcompton. 17.2.61.*

Table 203

KETTERING AND NOTTINGHAM

WEEKDAYS

Miles	180 LONDON St. Pan. dep.			
0	KETTERING .... dep.	4 25		
7½	Corby			
14	Gretton			
18¼	Manton			
22	Oakham			
26¼	Ashwell			
29½	Saxby			
33½	Oakham			
40½	Gretton			
39¼	Old Dalby			
51¼	NOTTINGHAM Mid. arr.			
67¾	211 DERBY Midland arr.			

WEEKDAYS

Miles	211 DERBY Midland dep.			
0	NOTTINGHAM Mid. dep.			
2	Old Dalby			
8½	Melton Mowbray Town			
22	Saxby			
26½	Ashwell			
29½	Oakham			
33½	Manton			
40½	Gretton			
44½	Corby			
51¼	KETTERING			
67¾	180 LONDON St. Pan. arr.			

SUNDAYS

180 LONDON St. Pan. dep.

KETTERING ....
Corby
Gretton
Manton
Oakham
Ashwell
Saxby
Melton Mowbray Town
Old Dalby
NOTTINGHAM Mid. arr.
211 DERBY Midland arr.

SUNDAYS

211 DERBY Midland dep.
NOTTINGHAM Mid. dep.
Old Dalby
Melton Mowbray Town
Saxby
Ashwell
Oakham
Manton
Gretton
Corby
KETTERING ....
180 LONDON St. Pan. arr.

Table 204 — ## LEICESTER AND RUGBY Weekdays only.

Miles	180 LONDON St. Pancras dep.										
0	LEICESTER London Rd. dep.										
2¾	Wigston South										
7¾	Countesthorpe										
10¼	Broughton Astley										
14	Leire Halt										
16¾	Ullesthorpe										
20	RUGBY Midland arr.										
10¾	50 LONDON Euston arr.										

Miles	50 LONDON Euston dep.									
0	RUGBY Midland dep.									
2¾	Ullesthorpe									
6	Leire Halt									
9¾	Broughton Astley									
12¼	Countesthorpe									
16¾	Wigston South									
20	LEICESTER London Rd. arr.									
19	180 LONDON St. Pancras arr.									

Table 207 — ## LEICESTER AND BURTON-ON-TRENT — Weekdays only.

Miles	180 LONDON St. Pancras dep.							
0	LEICESTER London Road dep.							
5½	Kirby Muxloe							
8¾	Desford							
12¾	Bagworth & Ellistown							
16	Coalville Town							
21¾	Ashby-de-la-Zouch							
23¾	Moira							
26	Gresley							
30½	BURTON-ON-TRENT arr.							
44½	106 UTTOXETER							
—	106 STOKE-ON-TRENT							
41¼	181 DERBY Midland							

Miles	181 DERBY Midland dep.						
—	106 STOKE-ON-TRENT						
—	106 UTTOXETER						
0	BURTON-ON-TRENT dep.						
4½	Gresley						
9¾	Moira						
—	Ashby-de-la-Zouch						
14¾	Coalville Town						
18	Bagworth & Ellistown						
22½	Desford						
25½	Kirby Muxloe						
30½	LEICESTER London Road arr.						
129¾	180 LONDON St. Pancras arr.						